Reading about fun activites at the SUPERMARKET to develop vocabulary, practice writing and enjoy coloring and other preschool and early learning activites for ages 3-7 years.

Bread Told ME

Reading about fun activites at the SUPERMARKET to develop vocabulary, practice writing and enjoy coloring and other preschool and early learning activites for ages 3-7 years.

Parent/Teacher Guide

For ages 3 and 4, read actively, pointing and demonstrating to engage the child's imagination showing them the pictures so that they can associate images with words.

For ages 4-7 still read to and with the child and encourage active participation by letting them say the words they recognize. This increases word recognition and soon the child will know most of the words and will attempt to read independently. Spend at least 15 minutes a day reading with the child to foster the love of reading and ignite their imagination.

The content is based on simple children's growing experiences. They are designed according to early language learning developmental milestones for ages 3 to 7 years. The workbook section is ideal for ages 5-7 years. Ages 3-5 can do the coloring and get more of these coloring activities as indicated below.

When helping the child with coloring, it is best to allow the child to express their preference for colors. In due course they will understand the use of appropriate colors, but it is not necessary. Art is self expression. To give your child more fun activities , download them FREE at www.rhodespublishers.com.

Bread Told ME

(at the Supermarket)

My trip to the supermarket was funny.

It all started when I found Butter asleep under the bread in a bin.

I asked Bread why Butter was sleeping there. Bread said to me, "Please help put him back in the refrigerator before he melts away. I will tell you the whole story later."

So, I called someone to move Butter to the refrigerator.

Then I picked up Bread because I was going to make sandwiches for my picnic at the park later that day.

This is all the food we needed to buy.

Bread asked me for the list of food
I wanted to buy. But I had it all in my mind.

I told her I needed cheese, eggs, milk,
cereal and a lot of other stuff.

Bread said not to worry, she knew
where everything was. She said she was
going to help me because she knew
what went together nicely to make a great picnic.

Bread said we must first pick up cheese.
Milk and eggs were close by so we got them too.
She told me we should pick up Butter
last to give him time to get cooler and firm.

Bread told me the story of why
Butter had been in the bread bin.

She said they had a party and Butter fell asleep.
No one came to take him back to the refrigerator.

After we picked up milk we saw cereal
not too faraway. So we picked up cereal and
then headed to the meat section.

Bread said we should get some
burger meat and hot dogs.
I was amazed how smart Bread was.

Bread told me that she was the
favorite in most families and knew the
best foods that were good to eat together.

We could not reach burger meat so we had to get my parents to help.

We headed to the vegetable section where they were shopping.

Bread said to get some lettuce and tomatoes for the sandwiches.

VEGETABLES

Bread said to get some lettuce and tomatoes for the sandwiches.

FRUIT AND JUICES

At the fruit section we picked up bananas, apples and watermelon. Bread said those were perfect to have at the picnic.

So we headed to my favorite section
where there were snacks and desserts.

Bread was not happy and told me to slow down.
We picked peanut butter and cookies.
Bread said they went well with milk.

Bread said not to eat too many cookies and desserts.
She said they could cause cavities in
my teeth because they have a lot of sugar.

I promised Bread that I would remember to
have only two cookies with milk to wash out
the sugar from my teeth.

I was about to get some ice cream, but
Bread said a fruit smoothie was
better and so we skipped dessert.

We left to get butter. Bread was
happy to see her best friend again.

We were done shopping. It was time to
go to checkout and go home to
make the sandwiches for the picnic.

Later that day we ate delicious sandwiches. Bread told us all about her parties at the supermarket.

She said because she is made fresh everyday, all the ingredients come to party with her as they are mixed into dough.

It is true, Bread is fun and a favorite in our families. She is very kind and helpful at the supermarket.

Draw an arrow to match the pictures to the words

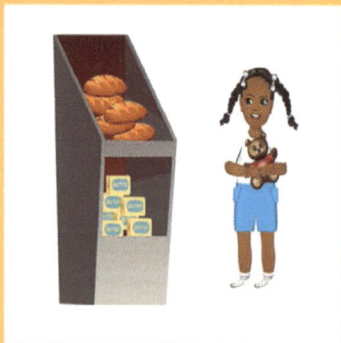

I see cereal and milk

I see bread and butter

I see vegetables

Draw an arrow to match the pictures to the words

I see cheese and eggs

I see alot of food

I see desserts

Circle the words of the pictures you see at the bottom.

A	B	M	E	A	T	H	A	N	T
C	D	E	F	G	H	I	J	K	L
M	N	O	P	I	C	N	I	C	A
G	O	C	F	R	U	I	T	E	T
U	C	O	O	K	I	E	S	E	W
X	B	A	N	A	N	A	S	F	G
P	E	A	N	U	T	H	H	I	J
B	U	T	T	E	R	A	R	T	O

Circle the words of the pictures
you see at the bottom.

A	C	E	G	G	S	M	E	L	C
C	D	E	F	R	U	I	T	M	L
B	A	N	A	N	A	S	O	R	A
C	C	H	E	E	S	E	D	E	T
E	D	T	U	E	S	D	A	Y	R
M	I	L	K	A	L	E	E	F	G
C	B	A	L	C	E	R	E	A	L
V	E	G	E	T	A	B	L	E	S

Trace the words

Bread

Butter

Banana

Meat

Trace the words

Fruit

Dessert

Cookies

Sandwich

Trace the words

Watermelon

Food

Picnic

Favorite

Circle the correct answer.

Answer key at the back.

Questions	Answers
1. What goes better with bread?	A. **Watermelon** B. **Butter**
2. Is banana a fruit or a vegetable?	A. **Vegetable** B. **Fruit**
3. What is better to make sandwiches with?	A. **Apples** B. **Cheese**

Circle the correct answer.

Answer key at the back.

Questions	Answers
4. What can make holes in your teeth?	A. Bread B. Ice cream
5. Where should butter be kept?	A. Shelf B. Refrigerator
6. What should you do if you cannot reach something at the supermarket?	A. Climb up to get it B. Ask for help

Find the letter that is missing and write it in there!

Word	Something is Missing
Bread	Bre_d
Butter	Butt_r
Cheese	Che_se
Eggs	Eg_s
Burger	Bur_er
Meat	Me_t

Find the letter that is missing and write it in there!

Word	Something is Missing
Fruit	Fru_t
Vegetables	Veget_bles
Banana	Ban_na
Watermelon	Waterm_lon
Cookies	Co_kies
Sugar	Sug_r

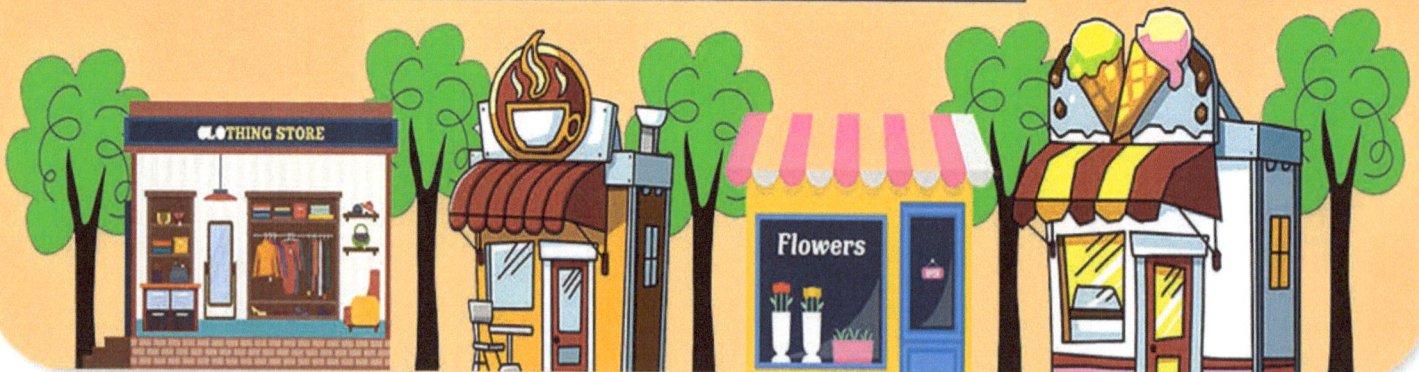

Find Your Way to Visit Cheese and Eggs

Start here →

Find Your Way to Visit Bread and Butter

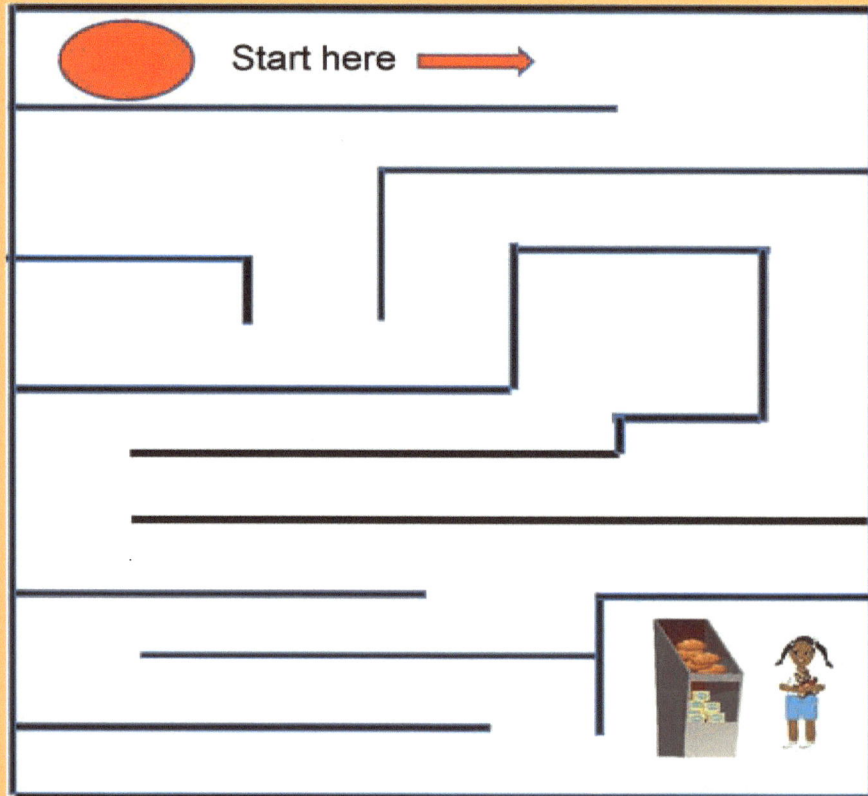

Start here ➡

Bread

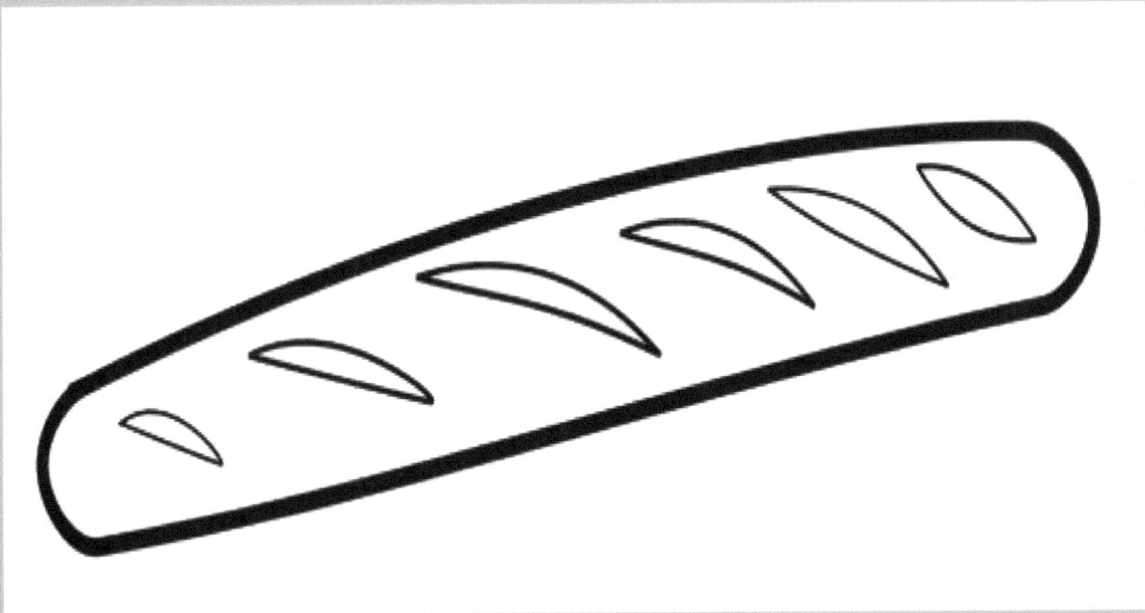

Food

Milk

_____

Ice Cream

_____

Cheese

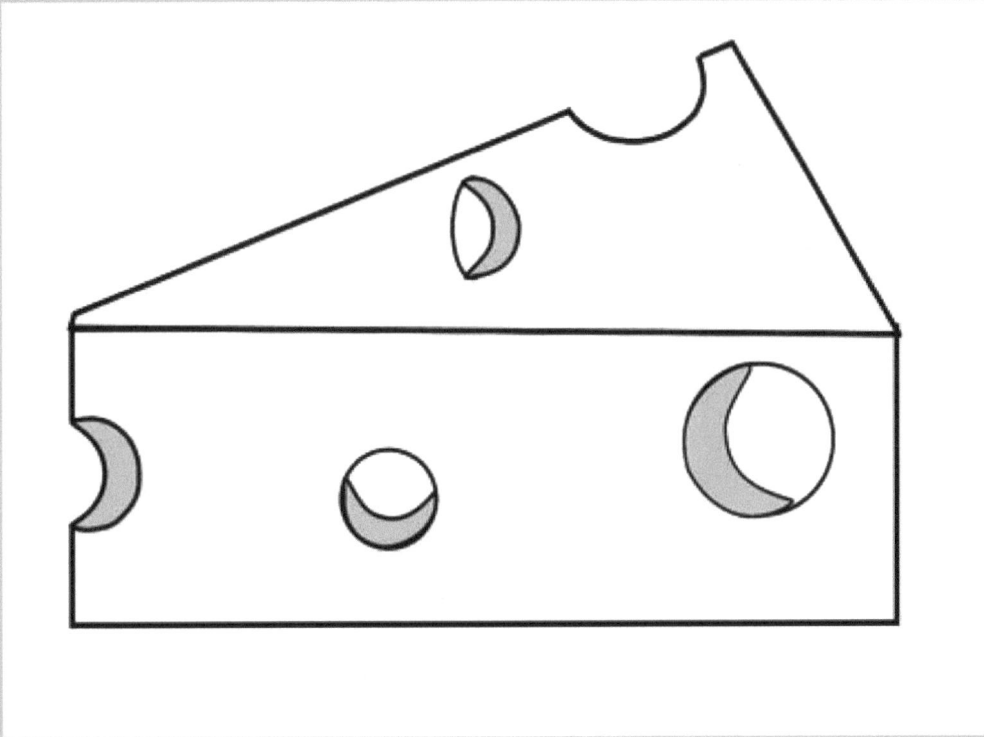

_____

1.	STORIES At the PARK
2.	FLOATING FRIENDS FOREVER
3.	SECRETS At the ZOO
4.	FUN AT THE FAIR
5.	BREAD TOLD ME
6.	MY DOCTOR IS LOOKING AT ME
7.	GOD LOVES ALL CHILDREN

If you have a 7-12 year old, avid or reluctant reader try: FARTSALOT DREAMS A LOT BOOK 1 and BOOK 2 by Dr. Florence Ramorobi – a dramatic story that will leave them asking for more. Find more about it here: www. rhodespublishers.com

Dr. Florence Ramorobi

Dr. Florence Ramorobi has dedicated her life to teaching and fostering a love of language, reading, and education in children from preschool on up. She is a longtime Education Specialist and has taught English as a second language to countless students over the years. She holds a master's degree in applied linguistics.

Her vast experience has afforded her the privilege and honor to provide education consulting services around the globe, develop learning resource material, and positively impact young people in and out of the classroom. Besides what she does professionally, she has added author to her resume. Her books are designed for children ages 3 -6. Her philosophy is based on preparing them for a love of reading and excellence in English language skills.

For more information about her and her work, visit her website at
www.rhodespublishers.com

ANSWER KEY

Questions	Answers
1. What goes better with bread?	**B. Butter**
2. Is banana a fruit or a vegetable?	**A. Fruit**
3. What is better to make sandwiches with?	**B. Cheese**
4. What can make holes in your teeth?	**B. Ice cream**
5. Where should butter be kept?	**B. refrigerator**
6. What should you if you cannot reach something at the supermarket?	**B. Ask for help**

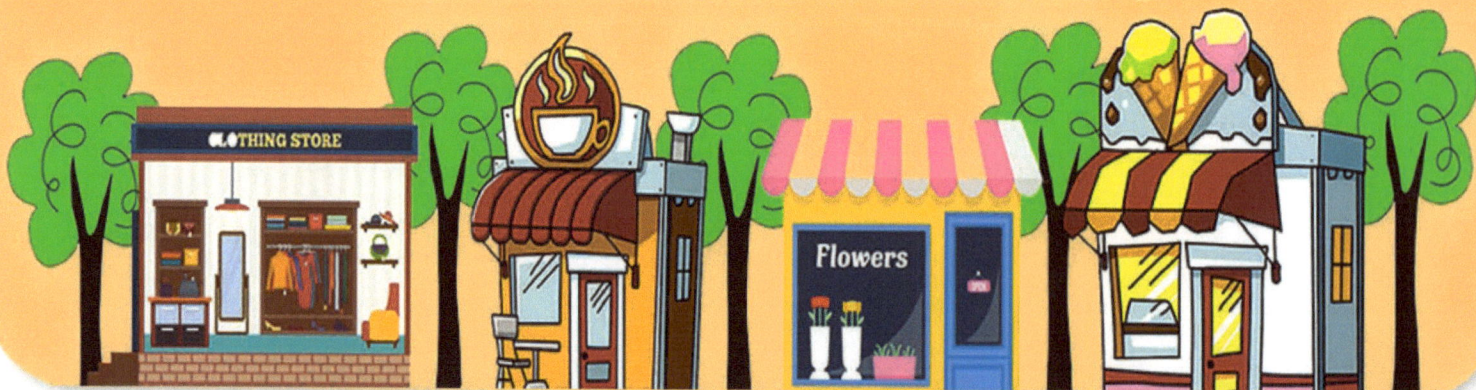

www.ingramcontent.com/pod-product-compliance
Lightning Source LLC
Chambersburg PA
CBHW041933160426
42812CB00105B/2638